# A MANAGER'S GUIDE
# TO PREVENTING
# LIABILITY FOR
# SEXUAL
# HARASSMENT
# IN THE
# WORKPLACE

Beth K. Whittenbury, J.D.

Other books by Beth K. Whittenbury include: Investigating the Workplace Harassment Complaint, American Bar Association Publishing, © 2012, available at: www.ShopABA.org.

# DEDICATION

This book is dedicated to my loving and supportive family.

# CONTENTS

# PREFACE

This book is designed as a quick read for managers, supervisors, and aspiring business students who need to know their liability and responsibilities with respect to issues of sexual harassment in the workplace. Where California law differs from federal law, the author notes the differences. If you work outside of California, the laws of your state may differ somewhat from those set forth below, however, most states follow federal law fairly closely. California, in general, has stricter guidelines than federal law. It's always good to work to the higher standard and not try to do the minimum required. Therefore, all supervisors and managers can benefit from a discussion of the higher standards applied in California.

All law is ever-changing and developing. Also, the commentary in this book is not case-specific. Therefore, nothing in this book can be relied upon as legal advice. For case-specific responses or for legal advice you should contact your own attorney or your company's legal department.

So without further ado, let's jump in!

# 1 WHAT IS SEXUAL HARASSMENT?

Sexual harassment is a difficult concept for some people because behavior that is perfectly acceptable to one person may constitute harassment to someone else. A person's motive for behaving a certain way is not a factor in determining whether behavior constitutes sexual harassment. Supervisors must remember that there is no "innocent until proven guilty" standard for sexual harassment cases. The credibility of the parties must be weighed in determining if alleged behaviors did or did not occur. Also, many people may feel "harassed," but the behavior they fault may not qualify as sexual harassment under the legal standards defined by the courts, legislature, or regulatory agencies. As a supervisor, you should address all behaviors that impact employee productivity and attendance in the workplace.

Sexual harassment is a form of gender discrimination prohibited in employment situations by Title VII of the Civil Rights Act of 1964. At the California state level, sexual harassment is primarily prohibited by the Fair Employment and Housing Act found in the Government Code of that state's statutes.

Although the Civil Rights Act was originally passed to prohibit racial discrimination, the law also prohibits discrimination based on national origin, color, creed, religion, and gender. In addition, federal laws prohibit discrimination based on age and disability (including taking time off under the Family and Medical Care Leave Act (FMLA), while California adds

1

marital status, gender preference and gender expression as additional categories protected from discrimination. So, although this book focuses on sexual harassment, remember that much of the analysis described also applies to the other types of harassment prohibited by law.

There are essentially two kinds of sexual harassment: 1) Hostile Environment; and 2) Quid Pro Quo.

Often, sexual harassment situations are very emotionally charged. So, to determine if you are dealing with one of these types of sexual harassment, you may find it helpful to take the emotion of the situation by thinking about the facts in terms of a formula. If A, B, and C are all present, then together they equal sexual harassment. **Generic Formula:** A+B+C = Sexual Harassment

## Formula for Hostile Environment:

So, for hostile environment harassment, what are the A the B and the C? A = unwelcome; B = sexual conduct; C = the unwelcome sexual conduct has become so severe and pervasive that it has created a hostile or offensive working environment. Thus, the formula is:

A) Unwelcome + B) Sexual conduct + C) So severe and pervasive that it has created a hostile or offensive working environment = Hostile Environment Sexual Harassment

## Formula for Quid Pro Quo (Tangible Employment Action):

We also have a formula for quid pro quo sexual harassment. Here we find that the first two elements, the A and the B, if you will, are the same as for hostile environment cases. So it is the third element that distinguishes quid pro quo from hostile environment cases. Please note that in either case, **you need all three elements** (A, B, and C) **before you have an actionable, legal claim for either kind of sexual harassment.**

So for quid pro quo claims, the A still equals unwelcome, the B still equals sexual conduct, but now the C is that an employment decision was based on the victim's acquiescence to the unwelcome sexual behavior. Thus, the formula for quid pro quo sexual harassment is:

A) Unwelcome + B) Sexual conduct + C) An employment decision based on the victim's acquiescence to the unwelcome sexual behavior =

Quid Pro Quo Harassment

Now, let's define each of those three terms in the equations.

## Unwelcome

Behavior may be unwelcome even if we intend it kindly. Again, the motive of the perpetrator does not matter. The relevant fact is how the recipient felt about the behavior. Individuals **do not** have to tell the perpetrator that he or she finds the behavior unwelcome. It is enough if they do not return the behavior, do not laugh at the jokes, make a face, turn away, or start avoiding the offender. In other words, body language counts. Even if no one sees any outward indication that the behavior is unwelcome, it just has to **be** unwelcome to meet this part of the test. In other words, the A element of the equation is completely subjective on the part of the person complaining.

In some cases it may seem that the person complaining is "too sensitive." However, **do not** substitute your judgment for theirs. Frankly, for this part of the analysis, what you think about the behavior is irrelevant. All that you need to determine is whether the person complaining to you genuinely felt that the behavior was unwelcome.

You will find cases where the person complaining engages in the exact same behavior s/he is complaining about with other people, but with this one person, s/he finds it offensive. Under the law, people have the right to deny certain conduct from anyone. For example, a woman might tell dirty jokes with a male colleague she has known for a long time, but files a sexual harassment complaint when the new guy tries to tell her some off-color jokes. That claim can be valid. The courts are split over whether other actions of the plaintiff need to be taken into account. However, whether the person complaining should clearly convey that the conduct is unwelcome will depend on the courts in your jurisdiction. So err on the side of safety and do not expect the victim to make clear that certain behavior is unwelcome. As a supervisor, you can convey this message for your subordinates, and your subordinates may ask you to do so. Once that message is conveyed, either by you or by another employee, the behavior must stop, or it will create a hostile environment for the uncomfortable employee.

In quid pro quo cases, we often find that what one party thought was a "welcome" affair later turns into a sexual harassment claim. Although there may not have been any outward indication during the affair that such a relationship was unwelcome, there is nothing to keep a subordinate employee from later stating that s/he only went along with the behavior because it seemed necessary to keep a job. This outcome shows why, even in states with constitutional privacy provisions, a supervisor should view dating subordinates as an extremely risky practice. The same problems can occur even when peers date each other. If one party has better connections with higher decision makers within the organization, the other can again claim that s/he only went along with the affair in order to better secure his or her position within the company.

If you become aware of a sexual relationship between two employees, know that the moment repercussions of the relationship trickle into the workplace, it becomes the company's business. Although in California and some other states, constitutional privacy constraints prohibit employers from telling employees they cannot date each other during their off hours, the moment that dating causes work-related issues, the employer needs to address it.

You may find yourself in the position of needing to ask employees if they truly welcome the relationships of which you've become aware. If they tell you that they do, make a note of that fact, including the date and time you had the discussion. Place that note in a confidential file to which only you have access. Should the allegation arise that you knew of the affair and took no steps to protect the employee, you can then prove that you upheld your managerial duties by asking the question and acting accordingly.

If an employee tells you s/he does not completely welcome the affair but feels compelled to continue, take steps to help that employee get out of the relationship with no adverse job consequences. In such a case, you should consult your human resources manager or the company's general counsel. Do not try to determine the steps to take by yourself. Just know that you have the obligation to seek expert help within the company about exactly what to do.

Note that welcoming behavior is different than consenting to behavior. The standard in rape cases is consent - did the person consent to have sexual relations? However, in sexual harassment cases, we use "unwelcome" as the standard. A person can consent to conduct that he or

*Put everything in writing.*

she does not welcome. For example, you can stay and listen to a dirty joke rather than making a scene by leaving. Simply remaining to hear the joke does not mean that the person wanted to hear it or welcomed having to listen to it. One cannot always easily leave a situation in the workplace. You need to stay there to get the job done whether you like what's going on around you or not.

Often, people don't like to complain even about offensive conduct. They don't want to look like a prude or a whiner. As a supervisor you should diligently watch the goings-on in the workplace. If you see something unnecessary to the work at hand that might be considered offensive, stop it. Don't wait until someone has endured enough unwelcome conduct that s/he is ready to file a lawsuit to get it to stop. We all hope that an employee would let you know their feelings before taking such a step. However, in reality most people will think that if you see the behavior and do nothing about it, that it would be pointless to talk to you about it. So be a proactive manager and save yourself and your company a lot of headaches down the road.

## Sexual Conduct

The sexual conduct element of our equation is an objective one. Would reasonable people agree that the scenario includes an element of sexual conduct? The courts have interpreted the sexual conduct part of the sexual harassment test to include not only conduct that is about sex, but also conduct that differentiates between genders. Remember that sexual harassment is illegal because it is a form of employment discrimination prohibited by Title VII of the Civil Rights Act of 1964. Therefore, if an employee treats men and women differently on the job, that differential treatment constitutes sexual conduct for the purpose of our analysis. Sexual conduct can also occur between members of the same gender, so don't just look for male/female scenarios. Courts have upheld cases were men have sexually harassed other men and women have sexually harassed other women.

In reality, courts don't always articulate the gender distinction in their opinions. Often, they seem to feel that where conduct is about sex, there must be a gender distinction in the facts somewhere. For example, this male boss wouldn't be propositioning his secretary if she wasn't female. However, in same-sex cases, the courts more consistently state the gender distinction. It is possible for females or males to be biased against their own gender. For example, a female boss may consistently make disparaging remarks about other women in the workplace, but never the men. In cases like these you may not find anything that you would consider "sexual" going on. Still, a gender distinction is being made and that can give rise to liability.

Clearly where the conduct does include sexual elements, the company may face liability. Consequently, conduct or speech that is about sex should be limited or removed from the workplace. Even if **you** don't feel that such conduct is offensive, it is offensive to many.[1] Remember workers can't leave the area without impacting their job performance and consequently, their livelihood. What does this mean you should do in a practical sense? As a supervisor, you should remove all posters or calendars of scantily-clad people from the workplace. Watch for inappropriate e-mails. Report offensive computer spam to the IT department. It is the company's duty to keep the workplace free from sexually offensive material or actions whether they come from internal employees or external sources such as vendors, clients or computer spam.

Don't allow dirty jokes. Truly funny jokes, which do not put down a protected category of people, are fine. You don't have to remove fun from the workplace, just harmful or offensive conduct. There are ways to have fun without offending anyone. Set a good example yourself. Be available for and responsive to any complaints. Treat all your employees with respect.

If you see or overhear conduct that you think might have offended someone, pull the potentially offended employee aside later and gently inquire as to how s/he received the comment or conduct. Even if employees express no concerns, remind them that you and the company are committed to providing a harmonious working environment. Make a note in a confidential file that you asked the employee about the conduct on such a date and make a note of his or her response. This will protect you later by showing that you did your proactive duty to uphold company policy. You should also let the company Human Resources (HR) manager know that you had the conversation so that if another manager does so as well, HR can see a pattern that the company may have to address. As a supervisor, you must constantly remind your employees that the company

---

[1] See Appendix A for a list of actions which may constitute sexual conduct.

has anti-harassment policies and that you are an open, committed conduit for complaints.

If you view conduct or speech that is potentially harassing, also pull aside the perpetrator and explain that the conduct wasn't of the highest professional standard and that you know s/he can do better. If you think the conduct was acceptable, but might be misconstrued, convey that message as well. Don't wait for complaints to come. Be proactive in creating a harmonious environment.

## Severe and Pervasive

When does sexual conduct become so severe and pervasive that it alters the original conditions of employment and creates a hostile working environment? That is a tough question to answer, because in most cases there are no clear lines. However, the Equal Employment Opportunity Commission (EEOC), the federal agency that regulates the application of anti-discrimination laws, has said that one harmful offensive touching of an intimate body area immediately creates a hostile environment. Other than that circumstance, lawyers and juries need to use their judgment as to when the line has been crossed. Being thrown against the wall and molested at work just one time would probably make most people feel that workplace has become a hostile environment. They wouldn't want to return or endure the behavior again. However, one dirty joke heard over the course of a ten-year tenure with the company would probably not constitute a hostile environment for most people.

This element of sexual harassment claims is an objective one. Under the law, there is a reasonable person standard that applies when deciding if behavior is severe and pervasive enough to create a hostile working environment. Ask yourself, "Would a reasonable person of the same gender and in the same circumstances as the person complaining find this behavior offensive?" Granted, this is not a perfect standard. Even within the same gender, people vary greatly in their comfort levels with certain types of behaviors. Try to find a middle ground and apply that standard. The "reasonable" standard has been applied in negligence cases by the courts for over a hundred years and appears to be the best we can do in our justice system, so do the best you can with it.

The good news is that you, as a supervisor, don't need to make that call. As stated before, be proactive. If you see or hear of inappropriate conduct stamp it out immediately. Don't allow repeated offensives. You shouldn't wait until offensive conduct has happened so many times that the offended employee hires a lawyer and files a lawsuit.

How you end offensive behavior will vary with the conduct in question. It is not always necessary to fire the offender, but in some cases, like grabbing an intimate body part, you may decide to immediately terminate the offender. Most cases require only a serious discussion and warning. However, case law demonstrates that where a serious discussion and warning does not stop the conduct, more severe discipline is required to show that the company is taking appropriate action. Your bottom-line obligation is to stop the conduct immediately, whatever it takes. A complainant should not have to make more than one complaint to resolve the situation. So do what you must to get the message across the first time. Again, most employers have a human resources expert on staff to whom you should turn to decide which steps would be most appropriate in any given case. Try to seek expert advice before taking any actions of your own.

Although the company's obligation is to stop any behavior leading to hostile environments, there are still things employees can do at work to have fun without offending anyone. Strive for a fun and harmonious environment where everyone is respectful and professional, but not too tense. One pat on the shoulder is not sexual harassment. Neither is a true, straight forward compliment. A compliment accompanied by a once-over might be. So, don't overreact, but do keep an eye on how the compliments, jokes, or touching is received. Remember, body language speaks volumes. So if the shoulder pat is constant and the receiving employee always pulls away, you should speak to the shoulder patter and explain that they should probably refrain in the future. However, if two employees start the day with a mutual back pat, and s/he are both smiling, that's probably alright.

Often employees and even supervisors mistakenly feel that company policy does not apply to company events that are held off company property such as corporate retreats or extended training sessions. A work-sponsored event is still work and all the same rules apply. Just because alcohol is flowing or you're dressed in jeans, you can't suddenly act unprofessionally. As a manager, set a good example at all times and make sure that your employees follow your example.

Remember too, that even if you do a legal analysis and decide that the alleged harassment does not constitute a sexual harassment claim, someone **felt** harassed or they would not have complained in the first place. Statistics show that most claims of harassment are not made up. In fact, many more people experience harassment than actually have the courage to complain. So if one of your employees complains to you, something should be done to alleviate the problem. Maybe a manager needs to undergo some interpersonal skills training. Maybe employees are not treating each other with the proper respect. Don't ignore a complaint just because it does not constitute a legal claim. Where disharmony exists, employees are less productive. See what can be done to alleviate the situation and rejuvenate your employees.

## An Employment Decision was Based on Acquiescence

An employment decision based on acquiescence to unwelcome sexual conduct is the third element of a quid pro quo or tangible employment action claim. "Quid pro quo" is Latin for "this for that." So, in order to have a claim for quid pro quo sexual harassment, something must be traded between the parties. The boss might say, "Sleep with me tonight and I'll give you a promotion in the morning." However, instead of using a carrot, the boss might use a stick such as, "If you don't sleep with me tonight, then I'll fire you in the morning."

Real life situations are rarely this straightforward. Sometimes a supervisor enters into a sexual relationship with a subordinate thinking the subordinate welcomes the relationship. However, let's say things don't work out, and the sexual relationship ends. Tensions associated with the breakup spill over into the work environment. The subordinate's next raise isn't as high as his or her last one. S/he makes a claim of quid pro quo harassment. How do you defend yourself?

Suppose the subordinate says that s/he never welcomed the relationship and felt s/he needed to acquiesce in order to stay employed. How do you defend yourself against that statement? Remember there is no "innocent until proven guilty" standard in sexual harassment cases. If the employer investigates such a claim, the investigator will need to assess the credibility of the parties. If all activity and conversation took place behind closed doors, then you will have a hard time justifying your past actions. Let's face it, a relationship between a supervisor and subordinate is fraught with peril. You are putting your job on the line.

Employment decisions can include anything to which there might be a reference in the employee's personnel file. These might include hiring, firing, shift assignments, promotions, demotions, job changes, discipline, and excessive absenteeism or tardiness. If you start documenting any employee, make sure that you document them only to the extent you do all your other subordinates. Treating anyone differently is a form of discrimination and sexual harassment is a discrimination claim. If you treat someone differently you have to be able to prove that there is a legitimate and legal reason for the different treatment.

Often managers will make decisions quickly without thinking them through. Maybe it just feels like the right time to change everyone's shift assignment or reassign secretaries. Be careful that you can articulate a legitimate business reason for those decisions. Perhaps you don't know about the advance some other manager made to one of the secretaries which was declined, and then the next day, you arbitrarily reassign that secretary. The secretary may assume it's a message that he or she shouldn't have rebuffed the advance. How do you prove that your decision wasn't in response to what went on with the other manager? You should have written documentation describing the legitimate reason for the reassignment, such as according to seniority it was that secretary's time to change, or the reassignment was part of established rotation followed throughout the department.

Federal law often now speaks in terms of a tangible employment action instead of quid pro quo. They are really talking about the same thing. However, we should know what the federal enforcement agency has to say on the subject.

The EEOC Questions and Answers for Small Employers on Employer Liability for Harassment by Supervisors says, "An employer is always responsible for harassment by a supervisor that culminated in a tangible employment action." The EEOC defines "tangible employment action" as a "significant change in employment status." In its enforcement guidance, the EEOC states that a tangible employment action is the means by which a supervisor wields the official power of the company over subordinates. When used as a method of illegal harassment, it usually inflicts direct economic harm to the victim employee.

An action qualifies as "tangible" if it results in a significant change of employment status. For example, significantly changing an employee's duties is a tangible employment action even if the employee maintains the same salary and benefits. Altering an employee's duties in a way that decreases his or her chance for promotion or salary increases is a tangible job detriment as well.

It doesn't matter if employees acquiesce to unwelcome, sexual conduct, or if they spurn it. Employees can sue for quid pro quo even if they received a promotion because they put up with the unwelcome conduct. The United States Supreme Court has stated that it is enough that there be a significant *change* in employment status. The Court does not require that the change be detrimental to qualify as tangible.

Questions often arise as to whether a threat of an employment action constitutes a quid pro quo claim or whether the supervisor needs to actually follow through on a threat before a legitimate quid pro quo claim arises. The U.S. Supreme Court has clarified that quid pro quo claims require an actual employment decision and that cases involving threats of employment decisions should be analyzed as hostile environment cases. In other words, are the threats severe and pervasive enough to make a hostile environment?

## Test Your Knowledge

The following vignettes allow you to see if you've understood and can apply the concepts we've covered so far. Take the time to read and think about them before looking for the answers and explanations in Appendix C.

1. Sally is a lower-level manager in a corporation. The head of her department makes disparaging remarks about females at least once a day. This manager says that women are dumb, that they work slower than men, that they are not as fun to work with as men and that they always mess up the company softball team because they can't play as well as the men. Once, when Sally was in the middle of a big presentation to important clients and the projector stopped working, the department head said, "Well, what do you expect from a woman?"

   Is this a case of sexual harassment and if so, what kind of sexual harassment claim would Sally file?

2.  Robert often tells dirty jokes to his friend and co-worker Al who always responds with a good humored laugh. Fresia sits next to Al and sometimes overhears these jokes. After a while, Fresia starts to tell Al a dirty joke every time she comes to her desk in the morning. Al finds these jokes offensive coming from Fresia and politely asks her to knock it off. Fresia responds, "Hey, I know you like those kinds of jokes because you laugh when Robert tells them."

    As a supervisor, you overhear this interchange between Al and Fresia. What should you do?

3.  Two doctors at a hospital engage in a sexual relationship during their off hours away from the hospital. One doctor is a former Chief of Staff and the other is relatively new to the hospital. Neither doctor reports to the other in an official capacity. After a few months, the relationship ends. The next month, the hospital board tells the doctor newest to the hospital that her services are no longer needed and terminates her employment.

    Does she have a sexual harassment claim? If so, which kind and under what circumstances?

# 2 RETALIATION: THE OTHER LEGAL CLAIM ASSOCIATED WITH HARASSMENT/DISCRIMINATION

In addition to quid pro quo and hostile environment claims, employees or former employees may sometimes claim that a company, its supervisors or employees retaliated against him or her for making a sexual harassment complaint. Retaliation claims are becoming more prevalent in the courts so you must guard against them.

To establish a retaliation claim, the plaintiff must first show that he or she engaged in some sort of "protected activity." In other words, an activity legally protected from retaliation. Making a claim of sexual harassment within an organization is a legally protected activity, as is supporting or refuting such a claim during an ensuing investigation. After establishing that he or she engaged in a protected activity, the plaintiff has to show that he or she was subjected to an "adverse action" because of the protected activity. On this point, courts tell us that the proper inquiry is whether the employer's action "well might have dissuaded a reasonable worker from making or supporting a charge of discrimination."[2] Finally, the plaintiff needs to show a causal link between the protected activity and the adverse action.

---

[2] Burlington N. & S.F. Ry. Co. v. White, 548 U.S. 53, 65 (2006).

So carefully watch the actions you take with employees who have been involved with a sexual harassment complaint. Reassignment of duties has been found to be retaliatory even where the former and present duties fell within the same job description. So has suspension without pay even when the employee was later reinstated with back pay. Unchecked rumors about or sudden lack of socializing with an employee who has filed a complaint may also qualify. As a supervisor you must do all in your power to protect those within the organization who exercise their rights under company policy from any actions which could reasonably be construed as retaliatory.

**Test Your Knowledge**

Please try to reason through these vignettes yourself before checking the answer guide found in Appendix C.

4.    Ally was recently named "Regional Manager of the Year" by her cosmetics company employer. One day, she and her boss, the Regional VP, walked through one of the department stores at which the company leased a cosmetics counter. When the VP saw the woman behind the counter, he told Ally to fire the worker and replace her with someone "hot" like the voluptuous blond he pointed to in a neighboring department. Ally was taken aback, but didn't respond and didn't fire the counter employee. Later, the VP asked Ally again to fire the employee. Ally did not complain. She did not refuse. She simply asked for a reasonable justification for the firing to which the VP replied that he didn't have to give her one. Ally did not fire the counter employee. Shortly thereafter, the VP started auditing Ally's expense reports and asking her subordinates to tell him anything Ally had ever done wrong. Ally began receiving below-average performance evaluations and was eventually put on probation. She went out on stress leave and ultimately quit, claiming constructive discharge and retaliation.[3]

---

[3] These facts are based on those from an actual case: Yanowitz v. L'Oreal, 116 P.2d 1123 (Cal. 2005).

Does Ally have a retaliation case?

5.   Two male employees filed a sexual harassment claim. Their employer hired a private investigator ostensibly to investigate the claim. Instead, he undertook an invasive background check on the two employees who filed the claim. The P.I. asked their friends and co-workers embarrassing and awkward questions about the two men. When the employer discovered this, it fired the investigator and retained outside counsel who then investigated the harassment claims. The two employees sued for retaliation.[4]

Do the two employees have a retaliation case?

---

[4] These facts are based on those from an actual case: EEOC v. Video Only, Inc., No. 06-1362-KI, 2008 U.S. Dist. LEXIS 46094 (D. Or. June 11, 2008).

# 3 COMPANY LIABILITY FOR ACTIONS OF SUPERVISORS

If a supervisor engages in quid pro quo sexual harassment, the company will be liable even if it does not condone the behavior and has written policies against such behavior. If a supervisor in California engages in or allows behavior that constitutes a hostile environment, the company is liable but may try to reduce the damages for which it is liable. To do so in California, the employer will use a judicially-created tactic known as the "Avoidable Consequences Doctrine."

Under that doctrine, the damages a complainant can recover in a court case are limited to the damages that the complainant would have suffered even if s/he had used the company's internal reporting procedures to address the problem in-house. In other words, an employer is not liable for damages that an employee could have avoided with reasonable effort and without undue risk, expense, or humiliation.

Under federal law, employers may raise an affirmative defense in cases where a supervisor engages in sexual harassment but takes no tangible employment action against the employee. Although the affirmative defense is an absolute defense under federal law which completely exonerates employers where it applies, the elements necessary to establish the federal affirmative defense are essentially equivalent to the elements of the Avoidable Consequences Doctrine.

The Avoidable Consequences Doctrine has three elements: 1) the employer took reasonable steps to prevent and correct workplace sexual harassment; 2) the employee unreasonably failed to use the preventive and corrective measures that the employer provided; and 3) reasonable use of the employer's procedures would have prevented at least some of the harm that the employee suffered.

One of the first things a court will look at to determine whether an employer took reasonable steps to prevent or correct workplace sexual harassment is the company's sexual harassment policy. A good policy will include: 1) a statement that sexual harassment is illegal; 2) the legal definition of sexual harassment; 3) a statement that sexual harassment is against company policy; 4) examples of behaviors which can qualify as sexual harassment; 5) a complaint procedure with multiple avenues of complaint; 6) a statement that any complaints will be handled as confidentially as possible; 7) a statement prohibiting retaliation against anyone bringing a claim or participating in the investigation of a claim; 8) the remedies available for sexual harassment; 9) the possible consequences to those found guilty of sexual harassment; and 10) how and where to report sexual harassment. Please review your company's policy and familiarize yourself with your company's complaint procedure.

Just having a policy against sexual harassment with these ten elements included is not enough. The policy must be implemented and proven effective within your organization. You can't have a policy, but not enforce it, and still apply the Avoidable Consequences Doctrine or federal affirmative defense. If a plaintiff can successfully argue that there was no point in following the company procedures because the company was not committed to upholding its policies, then the Avoidable Consequences Doctrine or affirmative defense will not apply.

What does all this mean to you as a supervisor? Basically, you are responsible for implementing company procedures so you must know, understand and apply the company policies against harassment in your workplace. If you receive a complaint, take it seriously and follow the procedures provided. If there are no procedures provided, you must still take steps to determine whether a remedy is appropriate and if so, to apply that remedy. When in doubt, contact the Human Resources Department for guidance immediately.

Keep the claim as confidential as possible. Avoid any appearance of retaliation in response to the claim. Squelch rumors where possible. You want to be able to show that you created an atmosphere that encourages employees to come forward with complaints. Maintain an open door policy. Respond effectively to any complaints you receive. If a case ultimately goes to trial, you want the jury to find that you and the company did all that you could reasonably have done to prevent and correct the situation.

## Who is a Supervisor?

Since we just discussed that in some cases, an employer can be held strictly liable for the actions of their supervisor, we need a working understanding of who constitutes a supervisor within a company.

An individual qualifies as a supervisor if:

A) the individual has authority to undertake or recommend tangible employment decisions affecting the employee; or

B) the individual has authority to direct the employee's daily work activities: or

C) the individual has apparent authority to do A or B.

Therefore, if you have co-workers making shift assignments, they might be considered supervisors. Also, if you have a peer review process, it is possible that those peer reviews could be construed as recommendations for employment decisions and thus qualify all those peers as supervisors for the purposes of assessing liability. Be careful to whom you give the power to influence or make employment decisions.

For the purposes of determining liability, any person with the apparent authority to do the above two things will also constitute a supervisor. Apparent authority means that, although the person doesn't actually have the authority to act as a supervisor, other employees reasonably believe that they do. For example, in some organizations, the lines of command become blurred and employees may not clearly know who really has the power to direct their work. Make sure the lines of command are clearly known within your organization and if you see or hear of someone overreaching their bounds, stop him or her immediately.

# 4 COMPANY LIABILITY FOR ACTS OF CO-WORKERS

In California and at the federal level, the employer is not strictly liable for the actions of the rank and file who are below the level of supervisor. The employer is liable for a hostile environment created by co-workers only if it knew or reasonably should have known of the hostile environment and failed to take immediate steps to end the harassment. Therefore, if a supervisor sees co-workers harassing each other or creating a hostile work environment, and the s/he does nothing, the company will be liable for hostile environment sexual harassment. So, you cannot turn a blind eye to potentially harassing behavior. Don't wait for a complaint. You must be proactive in handling inappropriate behavior in the workplace.

However, if the harassment takes place behind closed doors, then probably the company will not know about it until someone in the organization complains. Once you receive a complaint, you and the company must immediately act to determine whether the complaint is valid,[5] and if so, the organization must remedy the harassment. See the section below entitled: "Receiving Complaints" for a thorough discussion of how to receive complaints. If you do not appropriately respond to

---

[5] Generally, the way to determine if a complaint is valid is to conduct an investigation. To learn more about conducting investigations please see my book, *Investigating the Workplace Harassment Claim*, published by the American Bar Association and available at www.ShopABA.org.

complaints, the complainant can hold both the company and you, personally, liable in California.

# 5 YOUR PERSONAL LIABILITY FOR SEXUAL HARASSMENT

Although not necessarily true in many states and under federal law, in California you are personally liable for any sexual harassment in which you engage or which you allow to happen. Therefore, we are not just talking about your ability to do your job correctly to protect the company's financial bottom line; we are talking about your own pocket book. Yes, **you** can be sued! For example, Astra USA agreed to pay the victims of company sexual harassment $9.85 million and then sued about 30 of its employees for taking part in the harassment. Astra also sued its former CEO, who had participated in perpetrating the harassment, for $15 million to recover the costs of the investigation and settlement of the sexual harassment claims. So, you can incur the expenses of hiring an attorney and paying damages to the plaintiff and/or the company if you sexually harass someone or allow it to happen on your watch. Therefore, be very careful about the behaviors you exhibit at work. Make sure that you are acting in a professional manner at all times. Know your duties and your company policies. Abide by company policy and the constraints of human decency at all times. Refrain from dating subordinates or at least do so fully aware of the huge risk you are taking.

If you were raised that certain behaviors are acceptable, rethink that upbringing in light of company policy and the law as previously described. You must set a high standard for yourself and others at work.

## Your Duty to Keep the Work Environment Harassment Free

Employees enjoy the right to work in an environment that is free from discriminatory harassment. Now, obviously, that means co-workers and supervisors can't harass each other. However, it also means that third parties can't harass your workers either.

When clients, repair people, messengers or delivery people, for example, come into your workplace, they may make comments or exhibit inappropriate behavior. You may wonder how you can be expected to control their behavior. However, you must do what you can to prevent third party harassment. As a supervisor, you are responsible for maintaining a harassment free workplace. That includes prohibiting harassment from third parties who are not employees of the company.

Even if the harassment is coming from an important client and your company might lose an account if you say something to the client about his or her behavior, your obligation is to stop the harassment. Perhaps you can arrange to meet with the client off company property. Maybe you can gently convey your obligations and expectations to the client. However you do it, you must protect your employees. The post office will refuse to deliver mail to a house with a ferocious dog that puts the mail carrier at risk. You can and should refuse to service clients that put your employees at risk of sexual harassment. If the offender is a messenger, call his or her employer and tell them to send another messenger.

## Receiving Complaints

Employees have a right to complain to you of harassment or discrimination. In fact, you want to encourage them to do so. An open door policy along with prompt and correct action to end the problem is the company's and your first line of defense against legal problems related to discrimination. If you are proactive in addressing issues you see, you will have established a work environment where employees should feel free to come to you with their concerns. Now, what do you do when someone comes in and tells you that they have been harassed?

Listen compassionately and do not pass judgment. Do not say, "Oh, that couldn't have happened," or "I'm so sorry that happened." Both of those comments indicate that you do or do not believe the allegations. You need to remain completely neutral when receiving the complaint.

Avoid comments like, "I've known Joe for years, and I just can't picture that!" Please don't say, "I don't believe it!" Don't indicate whether you do or do not believe it. Try not to pass judgment at all! Just get the facts and let the employee know that you have heard their complaint.

A good way to make employees feel heard is to validate them as they go along. How do you validate without sounding like you're agreeing with them? Every once in a while you say, "So, you just said, ' . . .'" and repeat what you've heard without any commentary of your own. They will either tell you you've got it right, and then continue, or they will correct you. If they correct you, it's a good thing you checked. If they say you're right, they are acknowledging that you actually heard what they were trying to tell you.

If you find an employee repeating themselves over and over, you have not done a good job of validating. People repeat themselves to make sure that they are being heard. When you finally validate their points, the repetition will stop. You can begin your validation with phrases such as, "So let me see if I understand you correctly. You just said . . ." You can also say, "So, as I understand it . . ." Phrases like that do not pass judgment. However, do not say things like, "I think it's horrible that . . ." or ". . . should never have happened." Those types of phrases indicate that you have taken a side or already made a decision as to the truth of the complaint.

Remember that the complaint will be investigated, and until the company determines what actually happened, you can't assume anything. Consider yourself the guardian of a process and not an advocate for either side. The process includes receiving the complaint and getting it through the complaint procedure in an appropriate manner. You may need to talk to the accused, so it's crucial to maintain your neutrality throughout the process.

Once you have heard the entire complaint and validated the complainant, explain the rest of the complaint procedure. Usually, the next step will be to contact someone in Human Resources and they will start an investigation. Inform the complainant of what will happen next. Remind him or her that all complaints will be kept as confidential as possible by the company. However, **do not promise absolute confidentiality**. If the complaint is investigated, it will be talked about. However, the investigators should do this in as confidential a manner as possible.

Remind the complainant of the company's policy against discrimination and harassment. Tell them the company is committed to upholding the policy and that you will personally stay on top of the progression of the complaint. You might like to just hand off the complaint to Human Resources and consider yourself done with it. However, in one case a manager was held personally liable because he didn't check to make sure that Human Resources was pursuing the matter and the complaint was not resolved appropriately. Therefore, check back with both Human Resources and the complainant at least every other day until the complaint is fully resolved. Do this by phone or e-mail even if you are out of the office. (The manager held liable for not checking was on vacation for two weeks, but the court held him liable anyway.) Make sure that the company is consistently working toward resolution of the complaint and that the complainant knows the status of such efforts.

## Duty to Guard Against Retaliation

Since retaliation claims raise another legal risk, take steps to avoid such claims every time you receive a complaint. Before the complainant leaves your office, make sure that you explain the company's policy against retaliation. Tell the complainant to come to you immediately if s/he feels retaliated against in any way for having filed this complaint.

Now, practically speaking, although you and the company may go to great lengths to keep all complaints confidential, news will still likely leak out anyway. You must guard against rumors. In some situations, people will side with the accused. When that happens, they may stop talking to the complainant. This can be construed as retaliation for filing the complaint. Rumors may embarrass the complainant, causing a claim of retaliation. Rumors may also harm an actually innocent accused giving rise to a possible defamation claim.

These things are hard for you to control, but you must try. Keep your ears and eyes open. If you see or hear anything that negatively impacts the complainant as a result of the complaint, address it immediately. You may have to hold a department meeting, issue a memo and have private chats with people. Do whatever it takes.

Certainly, don't allow anyone to take a negative employment action against the complainant as a result of the complaint. Watch that the complainant's duties, shifts, desk location, vacation approvals, etc. don't negatively change as a result of the complaint. Make sure that everyone is treated fairly and according to the same policies. Remember that discrimination is differential treatment. If everyone is treated the same way, there is no discrimination.

# 6 THE EMPLOYER'S OBLIGATION TO CONDUCT AN INVESTIGATION

Unless whoever will form the ultimate conclusion about the truthfulness of a sexual harassment allegation actually witnesses the alleged event or behavior, the company must conduct a timely, effective and thorough investigation of the employee's complaint. The purpose of the investigation is to determine the facts of the case. An impartial fact-finder from within or without the company will conduct the investigation. Most likely the complainant, accused and all relevant witnesses will be interviewed. If you initially received the complaint, chances are good that the fact-finder will interview you as well.

At the conclusion of the investigation, the fact-finders will submit their findings to a company decision-maker. The company decision-maker will then review the facts as determined by the investigators and draw a conclusion as to whether sexual harassment occurred. If sexual harassment did occur, the company will have to decide on and implement appropriate discipline for the harasser and appropriate remedial action for the victim. As mentioned earlier, you should be following up every other day to determine that the investigation process is proceeding at a reasonable rate and that the complainant is informed of the progress. Make sure that the complainant is not experiencing further claim-related difficulties during the progression of the investigation.

# 7 WHAT TO DO IF YOU ARE ACCUSED OF SEXUAL HARASSMENT

If someone accuses you of sexual harassment, you may feel tempted to go on the defensive. Try to back up, and look at the claim objectively. Could someone have construed your actions as offensive or inappropriate? Were you acting completely professionally? If you feel the claim could have resulted from a misunderstanding, you may want to learn from the situation, admit your mistake, and apologize to the complainant.

Even if you believe you are completely innocent and that the complainant is imagining or fabricating things, you must cooperate fully in any investigation and act professionally at all times. Tell the whole truth when questioned. Check your files for relevant documentation that can substantiate your version of the events. Do not discuss the claim outside the confines of the investigation process. If you start discussing the accusation in an attempt to build allies, you may find yourself liable for defamation or other legal claims. At the very least, you will have violated company policy providing for confidential handling of employee complaints.

Perhaps most importantly, watch that you take no action that anyone could construe as retaliatory against the complainant or anyone involved in the investigative process. As difficult as it may be, if the complainant is your subordinate, you cannot stop talking to him or her. You still have to communicate with the complainant in order for both of you to do your jobs. Make sure that you maintain a professional relationship with all those involved in the complaint or investigation.

Refrain from taking any kind of employment action that will affect the complainant during the investigation, and make sure that any subsequent employment actions taken with respect to the complainant have appropriate supporting documentation and a compelling business justification. Even if the complainant is a poor performer, you cannot penalize him or her for poor performance without records documenting a sound basis for the penalty.

Again, if you document one person for poor attendance, make sure you are documenting all employees on attendance or whatever the issue may be. Even if one person sticks out in your mind as a problem, singling out an individual when others are also guilty (though to a lesser degree) can trigger a discrimination or retaliation claim.

# 8 REMEDIES

If an employee feels they have been illegally harassed at work, they should use the company complaint procedure. You should be very familiar with this procedure and understand its implementation. If the company determines that illegal harassment has taken place, its duty is to remedy the situation. It should stop the harassment and make sure that it does not recur. Disciplinary measures should be proportionate to the offense up to and including discharge. The company must also correct the effects of any harassment. For example, it can restore leave taken due to the harassment, erase negative evaluations, reinstate promotions or job duties, etc.

If the employee does not receive proper redress through the company's internal procedures, he or she can file a claim with the Department of Fair Employment and Housing (DFEH) in California or the Equal Employment Opportunity Commission (EEOC) at the federal level, and one of those administrative agencies will investigate the claim. The DFEH or EEOC will then either take the case on behalf of the complaining employee or issue the employee a right-to-sue letter. Once employees receive a right to sue letter, they can hire an attorney and sue the company. They may even sue you. That is why you must make sure to remedy all legitimate claims of harassment through the company procedures.

# 9 OTHER STEPS TO CORRECT OR PREVENT HARASSMENT CLAIMS

Always correct harassment whether or not a complaint is filed. If you see graffiti containing racial, ethnic or sexual slurs, remove it immediately. If you see inappropriate posters, take them down. A question usually arises about people who show up to work in "provocative" attire. If your company has a dress code, you should uniformly (pun intended) enforce it. Does low-cut or tight clothing give employees the license to harass? Of course not. However, your company's dress code should be designed to ensure professionalism and safety in the work environment. You can and should address clothing issues on that basis.

Another way to prevent harassment claims starts with the hiring process. Screen applicants for supervisory jobs to see if they have a history of engaging in harassment. If they do and you hire them anyway, you must monitor them closely in order to prevent harassment. Keep records of harassment complaints and check those records when a complaint is made or a hiring or promotion decision is contemplated. Such records should help reveal any patterns of harassment by the same individuals.

Continually monitor the workplace to ensure that all employees feel comfortable and valued. If you see something that strikes you as potentially offensive, address it. Either take it down, ask that the behavior stop, or inquire as to whether anyone was offended. Make sure any conversations you have in dealing with potential harassment issues are handled confidentially. Do not ask someone in front of others if they found something offensive. That puts them on the spot and may make them uncomfortable. When people feel uncomfortable, they sometimes also feel harassed.

Remember that the law is simply a floor for behavior, not a ceiling. If you strive for three things in your workplace: 1) awareness; 2) respect; 3) professionalism, you shouldn't need to worry about the law. Be aware of the feelings and reactions of others. If they seem unhappy, ask if there is anything you, as their supervisor, can do to help. Respect their answers. Employees these days come from very different backgrounds and cultures. Things they hold dear may seem insignificant to you. However, you must respect their feelings and make proactive efforts to maintain a harmonious workplace despite cultural differences. As a supervisor, it is your job to find a way for everyone to work together in harmony. Set an example for your employees through your professionalism. Always focus on the job at hand. How can employees do their jobs in a way that works for the entire organization? Make sure that you are always working to the highest professional standards and encourage you subordinates to follow your example. EMPATHY

# 10 OTHER ISSUES TO CONSIDER

In addition to sex or gender, the law protects other categories from discrimination/harassment. As a supervisor, you should know that the California Fair Employment and Housing Act (FEHA) protects individuals from discrimination or harassment based on the following characteristics.

- Age (40 and over)
- Ancestry
- Color
- Religious creed
- Family and medical care leave (don't deny it under legally mandated terms)
- Disability (mental and physical) including HIV and AIDS
- Marital status
- Medical condition (i.e. cancer, genetic characteristics, etc.)
- National origin
- Race
- Religion
- Sex
- Sexual orientation – including transgender issues
- Gender expression

Please be aware that, as a supervisor, you cannot allow any employee to experience work-related harassment due to any of these categories. Although some of these categories are not protected under federal law, it is best to work with the most inclusive list available. Even if a category such as appearance is not on this list, remember that treating people differently from others for any reason can lead to complaints. So, try to provide a level playing field for all regardless of any particular characteristic they exhibit.

## Transgender Issues

One area that managers are finding difficult to navigate with respect to harassment laws is the issue of transgender employees. Especially in cases where an employee is going through a gender re-orientation, other employees sometimes say or do things that could constitute harassment toward that employee.

California courts and the California Department of Fair Employment (DFEH) have recognized that discrimination against transgender and gender non-conforming people is a form of sex discrimination. Therefore, no one in the workplace should make comments or slurs relating to stereotypical notions of how men and women should act. The conduct does not need to be sexual in nature to constitute sexual harassment. For example, as a supervisor, you cannot tolerate or make comments on the way someone dresses, wears their hair or walks, because such comments can give rise to harassment claims.

Employees have the right to decide with which gender they will affiliate. Most officials suggest that employers allow employees to use the bathroom that fits their gender choice. Public restroom use is governed by a legal patchwork of city ordinances and state laws. San Francisco, Oakland, and New York have regulations protecting public restroom access based on "gender identity." "Gender identity" refers to a person's internal sense of gender rather than their birth sex. Where possible, establish a gender-neutral bathroom on your premises to avoid these issues in your workplace. A gender-neutral bathroom is one lockable room with a toilet and wash basin that can be used by either gender, but just by one person at a time.

When watching for transgender discrimination issues, remember that discharge, demotion, refusal to hire, transfer to a less desirable position, failure to use appropriate names, pronouns and titles, failure to allow bathroom use according to gender identity and harassment by co-workers, supervisors or management among others can all give rise to such a claim.

## Dress Code Issues

Remember that if an employee wears revealing clothing to work, he or she is not asking for harassment. Instead, you must treat inappropriate attire under your company's dress code. You may send employees home to change if you feel they have violated the dress code. However, make sure that you apply the same standards to men and women in your workplace.

Employers may not refuse to allow employees to wear pants on the basis of sex unless:

- The employer has a "good cause exemption" formally granted by the California Fair Employment and Housing Commission (or equivalent state agency);
- The employer requires that uniforms be worn as part of the employment; or
- The outfit required is necessary to the job such as a costume would be for dramatic roles or specific character portrayal.

## English Only Rules

Sometimes managers feel frustrated if their employees can communicate among themselves in a language other than English. However, you cannot force your employees to speak English in the workplace unless you can show that speaking English is a business necessity. As a supervisor, you can ask that your employees speak only English with you, if that is the only language you know, but you cannot ban them from speaking with each other in a different language unless that causes danger to others or serious interference with your business objectives. If you have a legitimate reason for banning all languages other than English during certain times, you must notify your employees in advance of enforcing that language policy. If you do not notify your employees in advance of your policies you cannot discipline them for violations.

Beth K. Whittenbury

# 11 CONCLUSION

If you know the law prohibiting sexual harassment, set a good example yourself, proactively handle problems and uniformly apply company policies and procedures, you should lower both your potential liability and that of the company. Remember, happy employees are less likely to sue. So, watch for and correct any disharmony in the workplace.

## Appendix A

### Guidelines for Recognizing Sexual Harassment

Ask yourself the following questions to determine whether certain behavior is sexual harassment.

1.  Would you want your child, parent, sibling, or spouse to endure the situation?

2.  Is the behavior job-related?  Is it focused on getting the job done?

3.  Is the behavior directed toward only women or only men?

4.  Can the behavior be classified as courting, flirting, or other sexual behavior?

5.  Has the employee receiving the attention objected to the behavior in any way?

6.  Has the behavior happened before?

7.  Does the behavior make it more difficult for the receiving employee to do his or her job?

8.  Would a reasonable person of the same gender as the recipient feel demeaned, degraded, or embarrassed by the behavior?

9.  Is someone using a position of power to make a person of the opposite gender feel inferior, vulnerable or victimized?

10. Is a supervisor predicating job-related status on receptivity to sexual advances?

11. Has behavior toward an employee changed negatively because the employee reported incidents of sexual harassment or participated in an investigation of alleged sexual harassment?

## Types of Behavior that May be Considered Sexual Harassment Depending on Their Severity and Frequency (the more severe the less frequency required)

**PHYSICAL:**

- Touching

- Holding

- Grabbing

- Pinching

- Hugging

- Kissing

- Patting

- Poking

- Brushing against another employee's body

- Impeding or blocking movement

- "Accidental" collisions

- Other unwanted contact

- Physical assault

- Rape

**VERBAL:**

- Offensive jokes

- Offensive language

- Threats

- Sexual comments

- Sexual suggestions

- Offensive sounds

- Teasing of a sexual nature

- Sexual propositions

- Whistling

- Continuing to express personal interest after being informed the interest is unwelcome

## NONVERBAL:

- Staring at a person's body or body parts

- Leaning over someone at a desk

- Offensive gestures or motions

- Circulating letters or cartoons

- Display of sexually suggestive objects, posters, calendars, graffiti

- Other sexually oriented behavior

Note: This list is not all inclusive. It is merely designed to present examples and guidelines.

Beth K. Whittenbury

## Appendix B

## Some Specific Actions Cited in Recent Cases That Can Constitute Sexual Harassment

- Managers putting knives to the throats of teenage female employees
- Placing employees in police-style restraint holds
- Comments on the bodies of and leering at employees and/or customers
- Repeated inquiries as to whether employees would have sex with customers
- Inappropriate touching
- Use of extreme profanity
- Promotion of supervisors who engaged in above-listed activities
- Stalking-type behavior
- Persistent requests for dates
- Pornographic photographs in the workplace
- Obscene jokes
- Sexual propositions
- Groping
- Sexual assault

## Appendix C

### Answers and Explanations to Vignettes

**Vignette 1:** If you said that Sally could file a hostile environment sexual harassment claim based on the facts, you answered correctly. We can eliminate a quid pro quo claim because the facts did not include any kind of employment decision. Although most women within the organization might view their chances for promotion within that department dismal at best, so far, under the facts given, no one has been denied a promotion based on gender.

Let's review the elements necessary for a sexual harassment claim. First, was there sexual conduct? Now, you may be thinking that there was nothing sexual at all in this vignette. That's true. However, remember that we made the point earlier that for the "sexual conduct" element we are looking first and foremost for a gender distinction because sexual harassment is a form of sex discrimination. Here, the department head clearly makes a distinction between men and women.

Note that I did not identify the gender of the department head. Does it matter? No. The courts recognize both male-on-male and female-on-female sexual harassment where the plaintiff can prove a gender distinction. Sometimes female managers have a low estimation of their own gender, themselves excluded perhaps. However, if a woman makes the workplace intolerable for other women, but not men, then we have met our sexual conduct element.

Next, was the sexual conduct, the repetitious comments, unwelcome to Sally? It would be hard to imagine Sally appreciating those comments, so it's probably safe to say that they were unwelcome to her since even by an objective standard they would be unwelcome to all women wishing to advance in the workplace.

Finally, for hostile environment, we need to find that a reasonable woman in the same set of circumstances would find that these repetitious comments create a hostile or offensive working environment. Would a reasonable woman feel that there was no hope for advancement in this department? I think most of us would agree that's exactly how she'd feel, especially when humiliated in front of clients during a presentation.

So, it appears that this vignette meets all the requirements of a hostile environment claim. Would Sally actually win in court? That would depend on the jury chosen. However, you can clearly see how this department head is putting the company and him or herself at risk of a lawsuit though this behavior.

**Vignette 2:** Here we have unwelcome, sexual conduct. The dirty jokes are the sexual conduct and Al has made it clear to Fresia that it is unwelcome coming from her. Remember that Al has the right to appreciate conduct from one person and not from another. Here, he's okay with his friend Robert telling him dirty jokes, but he doesn't like it from Fresia. That's his prerogative, but in some jurisdictions he does have an obligation to make that clear to Fresia, which he does.

Now, as a supervisor who is aware of this situation, you should take advantage of this opportunity to show employees both that you know and uphold company policies. Take Fresia aside and let her know that you witnessed the interchange. Remind her of the company sexual harassment policies and make it clear to her that since Al has requested she stop that behavior toward him, that she must stop. Let her know that you will also be talking to Al and asking him to let you know if there are any further incidents like this between the two of them.

Then talk to Al. Let him know that you overheard the interchange and have already spoken to Fresia. Ask him to let you know if she tells him any further dirty jokes because you have now directly asked her not to do so. You may also let Al and Robert know that it would be best for them to refrain from telling such jokes at work since it is clearly sending the wrong message to employees. Clearly Fresia overheard them, so others could too. Just because Fresia seemed to welcome the jokes doesn't mean that they might not be offending others. It's best if they limit such friendly discussions to their own time off company property.

Although this incident is at too low a level to warrant placing any type of formal reprimand in anyone's file, make sure that you tell your HR representative about it. This time you overheard it, but next time a different supervisor may. If there is no central clearinghouse for incidents that allows the company to keep track, this could go on for quite some time without the company realizing that each time is not the first time, but instead a series of events noticed by different supervisors each time.

**Vignette 3:** This looks like a potential case of quid pro quo sexual harassment – right? We clearly have the "tangible employment action" – she was fired. However, let's go through all the elements.

First, was there sexual conduct? Clearly, yes there was between the two doctors. They had a sexual affair. Second, was the affair welcome? Here we don't really know, do we?

The first doctor is a former Chief of Staff. Clearly, he knows and has worked closely with the hospital's board members. He is likely held in high regard by the board. The new doctor has no track record with the board. She could have felt that things would go better with her at the hospital if she acquiesced to the wishes of the former Chief of Staff. If she raises this point and says that the affair was consensual, but not welcome, how can the Chief of Staff or the hospital prove otherwise? She can claim that she was afraid that if the relationship ended, her job would be jeopardized. In fact, it appears that is exactly what happened. Within a month of the relationship ending, she lost her job, clearly an employment decision and job detriment – the final element needed for a quid pro quo claim.

Even if the former Chief of Staff didn't ask the board to remove her because her presence made him uncomfortable now that the relationship was over, how does the hospital prove a negative like that? The situation looks bad for the employer and it's possible that all the criteria of a sexual harassment case exist so, ultimately, a jury will decide. You can see how such a situation can end as a sexual harassment lawsuit.

**Vignette 4:** To have a legitimate retaliation claim, Ally must show that she first engaged in some form of protected activity. Now clearly, had Ally filed a complaint about her VP stating that he had asked her to do something illegal, filing that claim would have been "protected activity." However, Ally never made a complaint; she never even refused to fire the counter employee. All she ever said on the subject was to request a legitimate reason to fire the person. The cosmetic company's attorney could probably argue that Ally, in fact, didn't act at all. However, the court found that simply not acting when inaction is based on a reasonable belief that the requested action is illegal counts as "protected activity" under the law. Further, appearance is not a category protected from discrimination under the law and one could argue that a cosmetics company has a legitimate business interest in their counter employee's appearance. Again, the court said that even though there is no actual law prohibiting appearance discrimination, most people would probably think one exists. Therefore, the court found that all the plaintiff needs to show in a retaliation case is a reasonable, good faith belief that he or she is acting in accordance with the law to meet the first criteria of a retaliation case, namely "protected activity."

Next, Ally needs to show an adverse action taken against her. Clearly monitoring her expense reports while not doing that to anyone else, asking her subordinates for dirt on her, and lowering her performance ratings as a result qualify as adverse actions.

Finally, the court or jury must find a causal link between the protected activity and the adverse action for the plaintiff to establish a case for retaliation. Courts usually look for a close nexus in time between the protected activity and the adverse action to help establish this prong. In the vignette, the VP started auditing Ally's expense reports and talking to her subordinates shortly after she failed to fire the counter employee. The situation looks bad for the employer. Can they defend themselves at all?

If you understand this case as explained above, you see that the only place the employer can defend itself is with respect to the third and final prong – the causal connection criteria. However, as a supervisor, you can't control what's in someone else's head. Remember that one of the rules of this vignette is that the employee doesn't have to tell you that s/he thinks s/he is engaging in protected activity. So you simply can't defend yourself or the company based on that first prong. Next, as a manager, you will sometimes have to take adverse actions against your employees. When you do, make sure they deserve them. Before you make a decision that affects someone else negatively, ask yourself if you have a legitimate business justification for the decision. Picture yourself on the witness stand explaining your action to the jury. If you see them all nodding along with you, indicating that they would have done the same thing, then go ahead and make the decision, but document your reasons why it was justified by business reasons. If you imagine a jury looking confused, concerned, or even worse, angry, then you'd better re-think your decision.

The only place you can really defend yourself is on that last prong – the connection between the adverse action and the protected activity. To defend yourself there, make sure that there is no connection between any alleged protected activity and any adverse action you take against an employee by checking that instead you have a business reason for the action. For your sake and for the company's, every time you take an "adverse action" first write down the reasons for the decision. That way, if it's ever questioned, you are ready to explain it and don't have to search your own memory banks as to why you decided to do a certain thing on a certain day.

In the case on which I based the facts for this vignette, the VP did not have anything written down to justify his actions. The court felt that his actions looked like a "witch hunt" motivated by the fact that Ally had refused to fire the counter employee. The court allowed the case to go to trial finding that Ally had made out her basic case for retaliation and it was up to the jury to determine the facts. (The names of the parties have been changed and the facts adapted to make the points in this vignette.)

**Vignette 5:** Here, the two employees clearly engaged in protected activity when they filed the sexual harassment complaint. Bringing a complaint, participating in an ensuing investigation, and even the state of being a potential witness in an investigation are considered protected activity.

Was there an adverse action? Remember our definition: something that would dissuade a reasonable worker from filing a harassment or discrimination claim in the future. Do you think that filing a claim only to have a private investigator start asking your family and co-workers embarrassing questions about you would dissuade others from coming forward with complaints in the future? Most of us probably would. The court in this case agreed and found that even though the investigator misunderstood his orders from the company and the company probably didn't intend to authorize such a response, the background check happened and as such constituted an adverse action on the part of the company against those employees who had complained. Once again, there is no motive requirement for retaliation. The only question is whether the adverse action occurred, not whether the company intended it to.

This case illustrates that "adverse actions" as part of a retaliation claim differs somewhat from the "tangible employment actions" element in quid pro quo cases. In this vignette, the adverse action did not affect the men's employment. They still kept their jobs, shifts, salaries, etc. However, they were adversely affected by the company's action in their personal lives. So, you can see that "adverse action" is much broader than "tangible employment actions."

Finally, it is clear that there was a causal connection between the men's sexual harassment complaints and the company's adverse action. But for the men filing the complaint, the company would not have asked the P.I. to conduct an investigation. So, the final answer is: yes – the men would have all the elements of a retaliation case under this vignette.

## Appendix D

## Frequently Asked Questions

Q:     Is it bad to date a subordinate?

A:     *It's risky because you can't prove that it was welcome after the fact.*

Q:     If I'm finding a problem with an employee, can I start documenting his or her behavior?

A:     *Yes, as long as you also document all others exhibiting the same behavior. If you single someone out for documentation, this can be considered discrimination.*

Q:     Can calendars or pin-ups displayed at work, in lockers, or in a warehouse area be considered sexual harassment?

A:     *Yes. Such displays may contribute to a hostile working environment.*

Q:     Can I ask a co-worker out on a date?

A:     *Yes, but if you receive any indication that similar future requests are unwelcome, do not ask again. If the co-worker refuses your first invitation, you probably should not ask again.*

Q:     If no one in our organization is complaining of sexual harassment, how can we have a problem?

A:     *Often sexual harassment goes unreported in organizations because employees are too embarrassed or afraid to mention the problem to a supervisor or human resources representative. Employees also fail to report sexual harassment out of a reluctance to get another employee in trouble. However, these situations may escalate and lead to lawsuits if not discovered and handled early.*

Q:     Can comments made by customers to my employees constitute sexual harassment?

A:     *Yes. An employer may be liable for sexual harassment done to their employees by people who are not their employees when the harassment occurs in the line of work, the employer knows or should have known about it and the employer fails to take immediate and appropriate action.*

Q: If a co-worker wears provocative clothing, is he or she asking for trouble?

A: *No. Everyone has the right to work in an environment free from sexual harassment. However, the way someone acts or dresses may be an indication of whether or not they view some conduct as unwelcome. The more provocative the dress, the clearer the employee must state that they find certain conduct offensive and unwelcome.*

Q: If a worker goes along with my sexual jokes or also uses foul language, am I immune from a sexual harassment claim from that employee?

A: *No, not necessarily. Whereas, the court may take the alleged victim's behavior into account as a factor to help determine if the behavior was unwelcome, joining in jokes, or use of foul language by the alleged victim is not a defense to a claim of quid pro quo or hostile environment sexual harassment, nor does it excuse or invite extreme or abusive environmental behavior.*

Q: Can someone who has been in a consensual sexual relationship file a sexual harassment complaint after the consent has been withdrawn?

A: *Yes, if the person has clearly withdrawn consent to the relationship and harassment begins and continues in the face of refusals, the person being harassed may file a sexual harassment claim. Under these circumstances, the victim should communicate clear refusals to the alleged harasser and report the harassment.*

Q: Aren't most reports of sexual harassment untrue or grossly exaggerated?

A: *No. Very few actual reports of sexual harassment have been found to be false.*

Q: If one employee submits to sexual requests by a supervisor and gains benefits from the submission, can another employee sue the employer for sexual discrimination?

*A:*   *Yes. Other employees who were equally qualified and denied benefits may sue for sexual discrimination.*

Q:   Is the company liable for sexual harassment done by supervisors of which it is unaware, even if the company has a posted policy against sexual harassment?

*A:*   *Yes. The company is vicariously liable for "quid pro quo" (this for that) sexual harassment and the supervisor is personally liable.*

Q:   If no one corroborates the alleged victim's report, can I still discipline the alleged harasser?

*A:*   *Yes. The EEOC does not require corroboration of sexual harassment charges. The employer must take the action it deems most appropriate after weighing the credibility of the parties.*

Q:   What are the remedies for sexual harassment?

*A:*   *The first remedy is to use the company's internal complaint procedure as outlined in your company handbook and discussed during your training. If that procedure fails to remedy the harassment, an employee can refer the case to the DFEH or EEOC.*

Q:   As a manager, what do I do if I am personally accused of harassment?

*A:*   *Cooperate fully in any investigation. Tell the truth. Watch that you take no action that may be perceived as retaliation against the person filing the complaint or anyone participating in the investigation. Check your files for all relevant documentation that will substantiate your version of events.*

Beth K. Whittenbury

## Appendix E - Quiz Yourself

### Test Questions

### For the following questions please answer T (true) or F (false)

1.  If I am accused of sexual harassment, I should stop speaking or interacting with my accuser under all circumstances until the situation is resolved.
    T    F

2.  The three elements of quid pro quo or tangible employment action harassment are:  1) unwelcome 2) sexual conduct 3) that is so severe and pervasive that it creates a hostile working environment.
    T    F

3.  Giving an employee different tasks within the same job description can be considered adverse action in a retaliation case.  T    F

4.  The company must conduct an investigation into any allegation or inference of sexual harassment in order to gather the facts and fashion an appropriate remedy where necessary.  T    F

5.  Supervisors should have an open door policy for receiving complaints of sexual harassment.   T    F

6.  Sexual harassment is a form of gender discrimination. T    F

7.  You should always guarantee absolute confidentiality to an employee complaining of sexual harassment.  T    F

8.  If I see something questionable, but no one complains, as a supervisor, I don't have to do anything. T    F

9.  The company is not responsible when co-workers ostracize an employee who has filed a sexual harassment complaint.  T    F

10. In California, supervisors are personally liable for their own acts of sexual harassment as well as the acts of subordinates that they knowingly allow. T    F

11. The company is strictly liable (automatically liable) for hostile environments created by co-workers.  T    F

12. When an employee comes to you with a complaint, you should agree with them immediately.  T    F

13. Once you have forwarded a complaint to HR or a higher authority, you have done your job and can forget about it.  T    F

14. There is no risk to having a romantic relationship with a subordinate as long as it is consensual.  T    F

15. If the harasser is a client and not an employee, I don't have to do anything.  T    F

16. I should remain neutral when receiving a complaint even if I think it's a false claim.  T    F

17. Dirty jokes sent around the company by e-mail can never create a hostile environment claim.  T    F

18. If someone has experienced sexual harassment they do not need to report it internally or to an administrative agency before filing a lawsuit.  T    F

19. If an employee does not receive satisfaction when filing an internal complaint with the company, they can then file a claim with the DFEH.  T    F

20. The three things a plaintiff has to initially establish to bring a retaliation claim in court are: 1) protected activity; 2) adverse action; 3) a causal link between 1 and 2.  T    F

21. A male employee can file a sexual harassment claim against another male employee.  T    F

22. If an employee's concerns about sexual harassment seem unreasonable to you, you can ignore them.  T    F

23. If an employer has a policy against sexual harassment, but fails to enforce it, the employer can use the "Avoidable Consequences Doctrine."  T    F

**24.** A potential witness in a sexual harassment complaint cannot file a retaliation claim based on his or her potential witness status.  T    F

**25.** Courts have recognized that discrimination against transgender and gender non-conforming people is a form of sex discrimination. T    F

Beth K. Whittenbury

## QUIZ ANSWER KEY

1. False
2. False
3. True
4. True
5. True
6. True
7. False
8. False
9. False
10. True
11. False
12. False
13. False
14. False
15. False
16. True
17. False
18. False
19. True
20. True
21. True
22. False
23. False
24. False
25. True

Beth K. Whittenbury

# ABOUT THE AUTHOR

## Beth K. Whittenbury, J.D.

Beth K. Whittenbury has been an attorney since 1990. She began her legal career in the Labor and Employment Law Group of what was then known as Pillsbury Madison and Sutro in San Francisco. She left to found her consulting practice specializing in sexual harassment training, mediations, and investigations. Since 1993, she has dedicated herself to resolving employment issues without litigation.

Ms. Whittenbury is active in the American Bar Association, currently serving as Chair-Elect of the Employment & Litigation Committee for the Tort Trial and Insurance Practice Section, and has served as Co-Chair of the Public Education Committee of the Section of Individual Rights and Responsibilities. During her tenure as Co-Chair, the committee won the section's Committee Excellence Award. She is also active in the California Bar Association, the Los Angeles County Bar Association, and the American Association of Workplace Investigators.

Beth has taught business law at the collegiate level for 5 years. She has written three books, numerous articles and appeared as a presenter, moderator, and keynote speaker for several major conferences. Her most recent book: *Investigating the Workplace Harassment Claim* is now available from ABA Publishing at www.ShopABA.org and has made the ABA Best Seller's List. She currently conducts workplace training on sexual harassment and discrimination compliant with AB 1825 along with other types of corporate level training. She also provides executive coaching, fact-finding investigations, and expert witness services.

Ms. Whittenbury has been recognized by her peers for her quality of professional service and high ethical standards as evidenced by her election to the Fellows of the American Bar Foundation (ABF), a group limited to one-third of the top one percent of attorneys practicing in each state.

**Beth K. Whittenbury can be reached through her website:**
www.bkwhittenbury.com

**For More Information**

**or to hire**

**Beth K. Whittenbury, J.D.**

**To Train Your Employees or Investigate Complaints**

**Please Visit**

www.bkwhittenbury.com